D0453734

Freedom Has No History

Freedom Has No History

A Call to Awaken

Andrew
Cohen

MOKSHA PRESS 1997

Moksha Press Cataloging
Cohen, Andrew, 1955 Oct. 23-
Freedom has no history: a call to awaken / by Andrew Cohen.
p. cm.
Foreword by lee lozowick.
ISBN 1-883929-17-2
1. Spiritual life.   2. Life.   I. Title.
BL624   299.93 — dc21   96-77414

Contents

Foreword
by lee lozowick

I love paradox. After all, what is this incredibly complex yet stunningly simple affair that we call Life or Reality or Truth but the most paradoxical paradox that there is?

So here we are…a foreword to a magnificent book by Andrew Cohen, a book of striking clarity, forceful argument towards the only valid search, that for awakening, and a passionate cry for true sanity.

I first heard of Andrew just after he began his teaching work. I believe the year was 1987. I was giving a presentation (a fancy name for a talk) in London and one of his students mentioned that he thought I should look Andrew up. The demeanor of the man, obviously highly representative of his relationship to Andrew, struck a very sympathetic chord. I made note of the name Andrew Cohen. Years later when Andrew was making a presentation in Boulder, Colorado, I made it a point to meet him. Our first meeting was to be the beginning of what has come to be a deep and abiding friendship. But it is our second meeting that I would like to discuss. We met in a small restaurant, he attended by several of his male students, me by several of my female students—a perfect metaphor for each of our styles of Teaching. Andrew gave me a gift, one that could not have been more timely or more perfect. I had just been written up in the book *Holy Madness* by Georg Feuerstein, but I didn't even know that it had come out yet or that I was in it! This book was Andrew's gift. He had read it, and based on the material within, had a number of questions he wanted to consider together.

I have been questioned countless times by people who were ostensibly interested in my work or philosophy or whatever one wants to call it (the nature of the realization upon which my Teaching Work is based might be a nice way to language it). Inevitably their interest is some form of competitive aggression, or at best a self-absorbed attempt to "engage the Master in dialogue" or some such ego-based motive. What surprised and totally delighted me, not to mention encouraged me greatly, was Andrew's mood in this consideration. He was genuinely interested, passionately interested in coming to understanding or Revelation. He really wanted to know! He had no mood of superiority (I can hardly tell you how unusual that is for someone who calls themselves a teacher), no edge, no accusatory distinctions about the rightness of "his" dharma and the sincere but misguided nature of "my" dharma. He genuinely wanted to KNOW. I must tell you, I was *impressed*. The rarity of such a consuming desire to leave no stone unturned, no concept left unresolved, no knot left tied, unpierced, was not lost on me, no sir-eee. I am not known for suffering fools gladly. Most so-called teachers in our modern world have fallen prey to my chillingly revealing indictments. But I couldn't find such fault with Andrew. He really wanted to KNOW. We had a fierce, deep and enthusiastic discussion that day, and our budding friendship became cemented. We earned each other's Respect, an even rarer thing (when genuine and not simply defined by spiritual politic or cordiality of manner) amongst those who should be true peers of their dharma when it is true of them. But hypocrisy is definitely not rare in this business and most other businesses either by my observation.

Andrew and I have spent many a lovely afternoon together, made presentations together, taught together. I have enjoyed the fact that Andrew is not caught up in the game of spiritual vanity. He is willing to adjust his approach based on his ongoing investigations, explorations and discoveries. Ah, how refreshingly right. Truth is not some exclusive, rigid dogma but a living, breathing, ongoing adventure. (I may be mildly plagiarizing Andrew with that last sentence.)

And another thing now that I've got your attention. The depth of Andrew's concern for the liberation of his students is a very moving thing to feel. He really cares. He has no life of his own; no ivory tower saint this man. He is dedicated to the liberation of others. Of *all* others. After all, as long as there is an "other" how can the fact that there is only one, only one person, only *you*, as Andrew talks about in Chapter 2 of *Freedom Has No History* (a wonderful title for a book by the way, I wish I'd thought of it) be Realized? I'll answer that for you; it can't. Andrew's tireless dedication (just reading his travel schedule exhausts me) to communicating the depth of beauty, of joy, dare I say (okay I dare) love that he has *seen*, seen with his whole Being, is a wonder to behold. And I for one, am very grateful for his efforts. When Andrew sniffs illusion, laziness, denial, and abuses of trust and integrity, he is a raging fury of Truth and clarity unleashed. I've watched him do surgery on the mind of more than one deluded narcissist. It's a sight to behold, very satisfying for one such as myself, who has been attempting similar surgery for over twenty-five years now. (This is 1996, isn't it? Time, time, it does tend to fade into obscurity in this business.) Especially for someone as bumblingly inarticulate as I, Andrew's pristine dharma-words are an inspiration, to be sure.

Freedom Has No History may seem too "orthodox" for some. Andrew does not leave room to wiggle out of his absolute demand. There is no tolerance for options. One must be *serious*, absolutely serious. One must be committed, dedicated, passionate about this Work and willing to see the process through to the end with consistency, discipline, dedication, perseverance and perhaps most important, reliability. As Andrew says in the pages that follow, the Universe is depending on *you*. And why shouldn't Andrew speak with both such definiteness and such authority? After all what he says is true. Not because "I" say so (after all who am I—say, that's a good question, hmmm) but because truth is truth. It is what it is, beyond all of our subjective opinions, philosophies, biases, projections and expectations. The call for a practice of integrity is simply a call to a life, or Life, lived rightly. No life-denying asceticism here, simply a call to a full, rich, pure genuine life of liberated activity. This is a beautiful book. Truth is always beautiful. Read it with diligence and put it into practice. After all, only you can do it.

Prescott, Arizona
October 25, 1996

Introduction

Shortly before I started teaching, I was sitting by myself one night thinking about some extraordinary insights that I had experienced over the prior twenty-four hours. They were inspiring, uplifting, liberating insights. I found myself thinking about them very intensely. I wanted that penetrating clarity to return. Indeed, I desperately longed to have those insights again and because of that I was suffering. I was making a tremendous amount of effort while I was thinking about them, because as often occurs when something liberating happens to us, we have trouble letting go. It was for that reason that I was trying so hard. I was attempting through the power of memory to recapture something that had occurred only hours before.

Suddenly, in the midst of all of this I caught myself. "What are you doing?" I said out loud. "What are you doing?" In that instant of recognition, it became obvious that the striving to recapture what had occurred in the past was not only causing me to suffer, but was the very thing that was keeping me separate from what I had always thought I wanted the most—which was to be free. When I saw this, everything came to a halt. I stopped in my tracks.

Ever since that moment, I've ceased to look back in time to any particular experience in order to know if I'm free.

This insight in many ways was more profoundly liberating in its impact than the countless moments of revelation that I have experienced before or since. What I realized in that instant was that *freedom has no history.* This literally was a quantum leap in my own evolution.

"*Truly, freedom which is the insignia of the Timeless in the processes of Time can have no history, since all historical phenomena may be considered as the kaleidoscopic dance of the Absolute in the theater of the panorama of perpetual experience.*"

Swami Krishnananda
Rishikesh, India
November 12, 1996

Preface

Enlightenment is like a jewel and awakening is its discovery. When you come upon it, suddenly you realize, "I was so asleep. I thought things were one way and now I have found they are another."

Enlightenment is the discovery of a subtlety of perception that is profound beyond measure. As you pursue this shift in perception, what you discover is ever greater subtlety. It is always endlessly fascinating. Constantly turning that jewel in your hand, gazing into its reflection, you will see more and more and more. As you keep turning it, you find that the depth that is revealed there is miraculous.

If you want to know that which is true, you have to be willing to leave all of the delusion that you have accumulated and that so much of the world expresses behind forever. Only then can you stand alone, undistracted, finally able to bear witness to that mystery that defies description. When you are willing to give all of your attention to the pursuit of the Truth alone, you will find to your surprise that you have picked up the jewel of Enlightenment and are holding it in your very own hands.

1

An Overwhelming Passion

Question What is it that will destroy ignorance completely?

Answer Pure intention. The intention to utterly and perfectly liberate oneself in this life for the purest possible reasons. You see, when our intention becomes pure, our desire for Liberation transcends self-interest. One no longer wants Liberation only for oneself. So what ultimately destroys ignorance? An unconditional relationship to the attainment of perfect Liberation in this life, supported by an unwillingness to compromise for that.

Most seekers are satisfied with less than everything, with less than perfect death. The fact is, very few people in this world want to be nobody. Very few. Believe it or not, we can even be special in our realization. Competition between human beings takes place on all levels. It's not so rare for a human being to have enough motivation to taste what's possible, to have a spiritual experience. But it is rare when an individual has sufficient motivation to take them all the way.

If you truly want to succeed in destroying ignorance, you have to be willing to let your heart become so big that it breaks wide open—so open that you are no longer in the picture. If there is any attachment to being special left in you, you won't be able to do it.

Life is not a drama that occurs merely for our personal pleasure or pain. There is something very big happening here that is unthinkably important, much bigger and far more important than personal loss or gain. When we experience for the first time what pure intention is all about, that is when we discover it. Discover what? *Life as a whole.* We find in this discovery that in the whole we do not exist as being separate, and it is this realization that carries within it the potential for perfect Liberation. The fulfillment of that potential lies in the knowledge that the whole is the only thing that is important.

When this is experienced, one comes upon a kind of

caring that could not have been previously imagined. A kind of caring that is so overwhelming that it is beyond one's personal control. I'm describing a great passion, the purity of which completely destroys a merely personal relationship to life. If you want to destroy ignorance completely, dying into this passion is the way.

2

One without
a Second

Most people who are interested in spiritual freedom prefer to be followers. Very few are willing to make the sacrifices that are necessary to be free.

If you take a serious look at the human condition—the human condition means *all* of us you'll see that in the end there is only one condition and we are all a part of it. There is one person who exists and that person is who we all are. There is only one body, one heart and one mind. There is only one perceiver, and that perceiver is you.

Many exclaim, "There is only one." What they are referring to is a vague "one" that is supposed to exist everywhere. But if that is what one truly believes, does one have the guts to take it seriously? Indeed, if there is only one, then that would have to mean that there is only *you*. Very few are willing to take it that seriously.

When you allow this kind of contemplation to begin to manifest itself within you, you will suddenly feel things getting very real. A whole imaginary world will fall away. And then the question arises: if there is only you, what are you going to do about the enormous crisis that you seem to be in? Will you allow yourself to fall back to sleep? Will you pretend that it all really doesn't matter? Or will you discover that you, through the realization that there is no other, have the ability to change it all simply by taking responsibility for the fact that there isn't anybody else who you can ultimately rely on to do it? If there is ever going to be any significant change, it all depends on you.

I came to a point in my own life when I realized that I could not rely on anybody else. No longer convinced by what I was hearing from others, I knew that if I wanted to figure it out I was going to have to do it on my own. When I accepted this, when I no longer shrank away from it but instead came to a point where I finally accepted it, this decision brought with it a lot of peace, because I stopped looking outside myself for crucial answers. I no longer needed to look anywhere else for security or reassurance.

I knew then without a doubt that it was up to me.

When you arrive at this point in your own evolution, you take yourself a lot more seriously. You begin to take seriously the possibility that you *can* know, that you *can* figure it out, that you *can* find your way.

If you do realize that there is no other, that means that as a human being you will find enormous strength and inspiration in yourself, *as yourself.* You will stop looking outside yourself because you will begin to feel that strength and inspiration welling up from within.

When you realize that there is no other, it wakes you up from the dream of individuality. It wakes you up from the nightmare of self-importance. You suddenly discover that you exist as part of a vast and enormous whole, and there-fore *it becomes obvious that everything that you do always does and always will affect the whole.* Most can't bear to come to terms with this. But if you realize how significant your awakening can be, you will find that you don't have any choice. You won't have any choice because you will have given up the idea that you ever had a choice.

When you begin to take yourself seriously, it means that you also take the situation that you find yourself in seriously. That is when you peer beyond the sense of indi-viduality, beyond the illusion of separation and isolation, and begin to take seriously the realization of the fact that *you are that one without a second.* You then experience the great paradox. On one hand, you are a human being who seems to be insignificant, just one among billions. But on the other hand, in the same instant you know without a doubt that you are that one without a second. Very few want to go that far.

Understand that the entire process of spiritual evolution, transformation and awakening is not a personal matter—it's an evolutionary matter. *When evolution occurs within one individual it means that the race as a whole has evolved.* So the only point is: can, will and does evolution occur, or not? If you are not willing to take it seriously, it won't happen. You will slip and slide along with all of the others just slipping and sliding along in an unconscious soup where everybody is blindly following each other's lead. That is why it is so important that the individual be willing to take themselves and the possibility of their own transformation deadly seriously.

If there is no other, if it's true that there is no other, if there *literally* is no other, then you have to be that one without a second.

3

A Stand That Is Immovable

I f you are serious about becoming free in this life, you have to be willing to take a stand that is immovable. If you are deadly serious about liberating yourself from fear and ignorance, you have to be willing to take an absolute stand in relationship to thought, to feeling and to time. If you want to be free, you have to be strong, clear and above all doubtless about what is important. Indeed, if you are sincere you have to allow the desire for Liberation to be more important than anything else.

Given the right environment and the right company it's not difficult to taste, even if only briefly, peace, joy and bliss, to know what it's like to be free from the tyranny of the mind. In that kind of experience it's possible to discover how extraordinary life can be. But the fact is, most who do taste this kind of experience fall from it soon after. They may stumble upon it once again, but most often it slips away as it did before. This is why it's so important to take an absolute stand if you want to be free in this life.

Life is so full of endless temptations and endless distractions. It is so easy to lose one's way. Five, ten or twenty years later one may suddenly remember and exclaim, "How could I have forgotten?" After so many years, we usually have lost touch with our inspiration, and therefore may have to struggle very hard with doubt to once again find sufficient strength of conviction in the possibility of Liberation. Now we may feel that we're no longer worthy and even question whether it's possible at all. This is why our intention to be free must be absolute from the very beginning—always stronger than the mind, more powerful than any other impulse or desire. Only then will there be any real chance of success.

It's one thing to start on the spiritual path. Many people do this. But it's another thing altogether to succeed in liberating oneself from fear and ignorance in a way that is profound. It's so rare, and the reason for this is that very few take the possibility seriously.

When we are ready to take the possibility seriously,

our life will change in a way that is radical only because finally we have become sincerely interested in what it means to be alive. That means we have become serious about life, we have become serious about death and we have become serious about love. No longer do we allow ourselves to be casual about that which is important. To succeed in liberating ourselves from fear and ignorance, an absolute commitment *has* to be made. That means one is willing to make tremendous effort if necessary not to be moved, never to waver.

When you penetrate beyond the superficial layers of spiritual experience and begin to see not only into the nature of your own mind but deeply into the nature of reality itself, everything begins to shift. Then the unknown is no longer just a word but has become a living fact of your own experience. It is at that point that the part of you that fears freedom will rise up and tempt you to back down. It can take many shapes. It can take the form of your best friend, of your lover, even of your own reflection in the mirror. "Go back. You don't want this," they will all tell you. "You must not let this happen. Please, please go back to the way things were."

Will you be able to recognize this for what it is? Will you

be so committed to the possibility of Liberation that you will be able to see the many faces of your own ego?

The only way we will be able to survive the endless storms that the mind can create is through discovering for ourselves that *nothing is more important than becoming free.* In that discovery we have to find a willingness to come to an absolute reckoning in our relationship to what it means to be alive as soon as possible. The sooner we are able to arrive at a conviction that is absolute, the closer we will be to taking a stand that is immovable. A stand that is so immovable, so irrevocable that no storm will be able to affect it. Only then will it be possible to be free.

4

Abandon the Future

Question Many years ago, I discovered that a part of me is terrified of being free. Since that time I have been waiting for that fear to go away. My question is: is there anything that I can do to make the part of me that wants to be free stronger than the part that is afraid?

Answer You have to be willing to make a choice. So many seekers are only waiting for all of their fear and resistance to go away. If you're very serious about this, you don't have the time to wait. You have to come to the point where you don't care how difficult it is. You have to get to a place where you don't care how much fear or doubt you have to face. Don't you see, you have to stop making *any* demands upon God.

So many seekers say they want to be one with the

Truth, one with God. But at the same time they have a long list of demands: "I never want to experience fear, I never want to experience doubt, I never want to experience confusion, I never want to experience frustration. *Then* I'll be yours forever." You have to understand that the demons of fear, doubt, confusion and frustration are not God's problem. They're *your* problem.

In order to find the kind of confidence that you are looking for, you have to be willing to make great sacrifices and you have to be willing to suffer. To find true confidence, you must be able to bear more doubt and confusion than you ever have in the past. Too many people only want the kind of confidence that they don't have to struggle for, that they don't have to make any sacrifice for.

The kind of confidence we're speaking about is never free. In fact it's very expensive. You see, you have to get to the point where you're no longer weighing and measuring what you're willing to give. You have to come to a place where you don't care how much you have to suffer for it, where you have no doubt whatsoever that absolute love and perfect freedom are more important to you than any experience of discomfort. Then you will no longer be waiting. That's why you'll be ready. Ready for what? Ready to abandon the future.

That's what true renunciation is. The individual is willing to abandon the future *literally.* And when we are willing to abandon the future, then we are ready to give up all hope for the future. When we have given up all hope for the future, it is then that we have finally stopped waiting. That means that we realize that a better moment will *never* come.

We are always waiting for the perfect moment to let go. We are always waiting for the perfect moment to be ready to respond completely, wholeheartedly and without any hesitation. It is because of this, the fact that we're waiting, that when that moment actually does come we are not able to let go.

When we ultimately find the depth of courage and the strength of conviction to abandon the future once and for all, we will discover a context, a vast and infinite context where we will know beyond any doubt that we are free. And in that freedom we will be detached. But that doesn't mean that we won't care. It means that we will care even more. Why? *Because we are not worried about ourselves anymore.* And because of this we discover the freedom to care far more than most people ever do.

As long as we are waiting, we will never be able to truly love. *Never.* Our relationship to love will always be selfish because we will only be wanting for ourselves. When we cease to wait there is no time for that.

I'm speaking about a way of living that is radically different. When I say abandon the future, I'm not referring to coming back to the present moment. I'm speaking about giving up everything. That is something very different. You see, it is in abandoning the future that we are released from the hell of a morbidly self-centered existence where we only want for ourselves and where we always need more — where everywhere we look, a materialistic relationship to our experience says, "What's in it for me?"

Imagine that you are orbiting the earth in a spaceship. Sometimes you leave the ship to walk outside. While outside you are attached to the ship by a cord. Out in space it is the greatest thrill. You experience extraordinary, unspeakable freedom. But you always know that you will return back to the safety of the ship. When I speak about abandoning the future, I'm speaking about being out there and cutting that cord. The instant that occurs you will experience the thrill of existence. You will experience the overwhelming implications of the fact that you are alive. The magnitude of that is more than most people want to bear. Most want only to taste it and then go back. I'm speaking about *never going back,* about going all the way in this life. And that can't happen unless you are willing to cut that cord.

5

Cynicism

A shocking cynicism is deeply embedded in the hearts and minds of so many of us. Because we have grown up in this rather miserable world, most of us have more than good reason to be cynical about the possibility of Liberation. But if our goal is a spiritual Enlightenment that is profound, then we must find a way to make ourselves available and receptive to that which is unimaginable.

There is something very safe about being out of touch with the possibility of true emancipation in this life. Indeed, it is not difficult to recognize that the fundamentally cynical stance that so many of us unknowingly allow ourselves to abide in protects us from the potentially overwhelming experience of stumbling upon the Truth.

I have seen many people fall into a state where

suddenly they find that they are awake, deeply in touch with the experience of being alive. A state where their heart has been liberated from its normal, very closed-down, cynical condition. And I have noticed that in most cases, the depth of vulnerability that was experienced was too much to bear. Indeed, to see that deeply and to know that much forces a depth of surrender that mercilessly challenges every single idea we have about who we are.

To be cynical means that we don't believe that it's possible to be free, that we don't believe that it's possible to be truly happy. To be cynical means that we are mistrustful of life and frightened of love. Those who are cynical find it impossible to believe in a kind of love that does not want for itself. Indeed, they do not believe there is such a thing as perfect goodness. If we want to be free, we must recognize that cynicism protects us from the deepest part of ourselves. It protects us from the unimaginable mystery that always lies within us.

Believing that life is fundamentally not trustworthy also protects us from having to face into its overwhelming complexity. The cynical stance always provides the luxury of not having to question too deeply. It lets us off the hook. But even more importantly, cynicism makes it very difficult to experience life in such a way that we will know what is meaningful, significant and profound beyond measure. That is why if we do want to be free, we have to find a way to destroy the cynicism that has been protecting us from having to be too vulnerable, see too deeply and know too much. If we want to be free, we have to find a way to face into life absolutely.

6

What Am I Doing?

If you look closely enough, you will see that we live in a way that makes very little actually possible. You only have to have your eyes open for a very short time to be able to see this for yourself. We create prisons and then we live in them. Look deeply into the nature of your own experience. Look at the way you're living your own life. Look at the way other people are living their own lives. It won't be difficult to see the degree of compromise that so many of us are willing to tolerate in the way that we live.

If we want to be free, then we have to come to the end of a fundamentally divided relationship to life. The kind of compromise that most of us seem happy to live with is the expression of the very division that has to come to an end if any radical change is to occur. But who has the courage? Who would dare to come to the end of compromise? Who is truly willing to no longer live a life of division?

If we want to be free we have to be willing to question *everything*. We have to be willing to question all of our fixed ideas. We have to be willing to look directly into how and why we are living in the way that we are. Because if we are serious, the life that we are now living has become a powerful expression of love and beauty. If it has not, then there are simple reasons why.

If you are truly serious, you have to ask yourself, "What am I doing?" Everything can be revealed in asking this simple question: "What am I doing? What am I *really* doing?" This question can enable you to come to terms with the most fundamental aspects of what it means to be a human being. Within a very short time you can find out how selfish or unselfish you really are. You can find out how interested in true love you really are. This question can help you find out what your relationship to life is in a way that has the potential, if you're ready for it, to set you free.

There are very few human beings who truly want to be free more than anything else. There are very few human beings who are more interested in what is true than they are in how they feel. Those few who are, will succeed. Anyone who is that sincere about this, who is willing to let everything else in life come second, will find their way through to the other side. Something extraordinary will happen. That which is sacred will engulf them. If they fold their hands in prayer, their prayer will have a power that others' does not. If they meditate, their meditation will become profound. If an undivided relationship to life is more important to us than anything else, then our own life will eventually become a living reflection of that which is undivided.

Usually when we ask ourselves the question "What am I doing?" what is discovered is not as pleasing as we would like it to be. Often we find that we are more self-centered than we had previously imagined. Through asking ourselves this question in a sincere way, the veil of pretense and self-deception will be lifted and we will come face-to-face with the truth of our own condition. It is only in that kind of stark reflection that we can see for ourselves, maybe for the very first time, how far we have to be willing to go for radical transformation to occur.

The reason it is so important to ask ourselves this question is that it is possible for a human being to believe many things about themselves that are not true. If we're sincere about coming to the end of a divided relationship to life, then everything has to be seen for what it is.

The question "What am I doing?" has the power to reveal the truth about our relationship to life. This simple question can help bring us to a state of real maturity, a place where we are no longer able to lie to ourselves in the way that so many of us are more than willing to do. Not willing to compromise means no longer being able to live with the pretense that things are other than they actually are.

So sincerity about the quest for Liberation means that we are ready and willing to face into a kind of raw vulnerability that previously was perceived to be literally unbearable. And in that vulnerability all fear, confusion and ambivalence can be faced in a very direct and powerful way. Indeed, the courage to dive this deep makes it possible for everything to change. It can be the beginning of an avalanche, an earthquake, an upheaval from which nothing will remain the same. If we are sincere we have to be willing to burn in the fire of our own destruction. We have to be willing to see things as they are. Finally we have to be unable to compromise and willing to express a fearless interest in the Truth. Then we will be ready to burn while we're alive and see what will come.

7

An Absolute Choice

There are times when suddenly everything becomes clear in a way that is profound, when everything falls miraculously into place, when the burden of confusion lifts and one is able to see the way things actually are. In moments like these one experiences Liberation.

Many, at one time or another, have experienced moments of Liberation, but few have been so deeply affected that their lives have become transformed as a result. Indeed, if one looks closely at the personal lives of many who seem to sincerely pursue spiritual teachings, often one will find much of the same confusion as there is in the lives of those who express no spiritual interest whatsoever.

Why is this? *Because it is not spiritual experiences in and of themselves that set us free.* It is not the experience of overwhelming love, unbearable bliss or even penetrating insight that allows people to change in an extraordinary way. What allows the event of profound insight and revelation to become extraordinary transformation is ultimately only the readiness and willingness of the individual to surrender unconditionally to that which is discovered in the spiritual experience.

One who is truly ready and willing to surrender, once having tasted what it means to be awake, will stay awake. If one is not ready to surrender unconditionally, if the context in which the experience of revelation occurs is one of profound attachment to the way things have been, then even the direct experiential revelation of the spiritual dimension of life in all its glory will not be enough to deeply affect that individual's relationship to life. *The context in which we seek is an absolute choice.*

Again, what allows the event of profound insight and revelation to become extraordinary transformation is ultimately only the readiness and willingness of the individual to surrender unconditionally to that which is discovered in the spiritual experience. Spiritual experiences in and of themselves do not set us free.

8

A Perfect Relationship with Thought

Have you ever considered what it might be like to have a perfect relationship with thought? If you want to be free, it's very important to understand that the expression of our spiritual attainment can ultimately be reduced to the depth and profundity of our relationship with thought. One who is liberated has a very different relationship with thought than one who is not. Looking into the question of what is a perfect relationship with thought is an important way of gaining insight into the meaning and significance of the enlightened condition. Indeed, if one dares to question seriously what one's relationship with thought is, the whole world can be turned upside down instantly.

When looking into this question of what is a perfect relationship with thought, it's very important not to be concerned with one's relationship with particular thoughts, but instead to be concerned only with one's relationship with thought itself. That means allowing all thoughts to become perfectly equal. It's an illuminating exercise to reduce all thoughts to a perfectly equal status and from there to inquire into the nature of what one's relationship with thought itself actually is. You see, as long as we give our attention only to our relationship with particular thoughts, it will be impossible to find that door, that portal through which we can discover another dimension of perception.

If we want to be free, then we have to find a way to literally leave this world behind forever. And the way to leave this world behind forever is to wholeheartedly inquire into the question: what is our relationship with thought? When we begin to question our relationship with thought, then our relationship with all of the objects that arise in awareness, including the world and everything in it, will be seen in a dramatically different light. That is because through a one-pointed inquiry into our relationship with thought, the limitless context in which all thought arises will be discovered. The discovery of that limitless context is the realization of the enlightened perspective. It is only because our attention has always been so narrowly focused on thought and the movement of thought that the context in which thought arises is not perceived. And because that context in which thought arises is not perceived, our fundamental experience of being alive is one of limitation.

Our relationship with thought is our relationship with life. Our relationship with thought is our relationship with the world. Our relationship with thought is our relationship with the whole universe. The relationship with thought is the link between the experience of pure, undifferentiated consciousness and the reality of time and space and the whole world of multiplicity that arises within it.

An ignorant condition is one in which we are more interested in thought than we are in the context in which thought arises. The difference between the enlightened perspective and the unenlightened perspective is simply that in the enlightened perspective, one is more interested in the context in which thoughts arise than they are in the nature of the thoughts themselves. That context is infinite space. Thought is time and memory. When our attention is rooted in infinite space, our experience is freedom. When our attention is rooted in time and memory, our experience is bondage and limitation.

This shift of attention from being fascinated with

thought to fascination with the context in which thought arises is the shift from being asleep to being awake. It is a movement from meditation on time and memory to meditation on no time and no memory. Always inherent in this shift of attention from limitation to no limitation is transformation. And transformation demands that all conclusions drawn about the nature of thought prior to the discovery of that context be reexamined.

Those who are more interested in thought than they are in the limitless context in which thought arises are almost always intimidated by the discovery of that context. Indeed, in profound realization, so much that had appeared to be significant is discovered to be completely insignificant. This can be terrifying.

One who abides permanently in the enlightened perspective is no longer confused by thought and the movement of thought. Because of this, they seem to be able to move in a miraculous way through the world of time and space. One who is no longer confused by thought and the movement of thought mysteriously emanates that which is limitless and ungraspable. Indeed, we emanate that which we concentrate upon. That is why one who concentrates solely upon thought and the movement of thought expresses limitation. And one who concentrates upon the context in which thoughts arise expresses that ungraspable knowledge of no limitation.

Awakening begins when one experiences for the first time a shift of attention from thought and the movement of thought to the limitless context in which thought arises. In the initial perception of that context, there is simultaneously the discovery of no limitation and the recognition that limitation had been one's fundamental experience up until that point. Awakening is complete only when the shift from identification with thought and the movement of thought to that context in which thought arises has become permanent.

Now one is no longer unduly distracted by any particular thought that arises in awareness. Now one is naturally resting in and as that context itself, not as any particular thought whatsoever.

9

Stop Struggling

Most people are lost in what seems to be an almost endless struggle. A struggle against the experience of thought. A struggle against the arising of feeling. A struggle against the movement of time. This seems to go on and on and on. There may be temporary breaks, brief moments when one experiences some relief, but this usually doesn't last very long, and then one begins to struggle once again.

If we can learn how to give up the struggle, we will discover a natural and inherent freedom that has been there all the time. A very big part of spiritual practice is about learning how to stop struggling. When I speak about giving up the struggle, I'm speaking about being willing to give up a very rigid, fearful and self-centered relationship to our experience. This demands a lot of courage. Because in spite of the fact that many people claim that they want to be free, most often when they are actually given the opportunity to stop struggling, they don't want to. They don't want to because the struggle, as unpleasant, painful and limiting as it is, at least provides a safe refuge, a familiar ground on which to exist. It is that place from which one can always recognize oneself.

If we are truly prepared to give up the struggle, if we are prepared to stop struggling in the way that we have been so used to, we have to begin to make room for what we *don't know.* We have to make room for what we don't know in relationship to our inner experience and also in relationship to our outer lives. The secret of Liberation is found through learning experientially what it means to stop struggling. And once we have experienced what it means not to struggle, even if only for a very brief instant, we have to find the courage to put that into practice in the way that we live.

Finding the willingness to stop struggling is one of the most challenging parts of spiritual practice. Indeed, it seems to be very difficult for most people to grasp the subtlety inherent in ceasing to struggle to the degree that it could actually become a natural state. That can only occur if it is something that one wants more than anything else in life.

In order to find out what it means to stop struggling, one has to be willing to look very deeply into the reasons why one is endlessly struggling in the first place. Not only do we struggle to hold onto blissful feelings, happy memories and pleasant experiences, but we also struggle to hold onto fear, morbidity and unhappiness. We struggle to hold onto what is pleasurable and also we struggle to hold onto what is painful. This is a blind, mechanical and very conditioned clinging onto that which is familiar.

What is revealing is that when we are lucky enough to experience what it's like not to struggle, even if the experience is a positive one, we are almost always threatened by its implications. When we finally do cease to struggle, what is discovered is a depth that is unknown. Ceasing to struggle and the experience of that depth is most often perceived as inspiring and intensely meaningful, but far too demanding a state to live one's whole life in.

One of the most shocking revelations that occurs in genuine spiritual practice is the discovery of how profound is our attachment to the known and how meager is our willingness to truly embrace the unknown. It is in that revelation that we see for ourselves that the very act of struggling, even if unpleasant, allows us to remain in territory that appears fundamentally safe and secure because it is known.

If we are sincere in our desire to stop struggling, we have to become more and more interested in being attached to nothing whatsoever except the perfect attainment of freedom alone. Freedom means peace, cessation, joy and bliss. When we come to that point in our evolution as a human being where we finally are ready to stop struggling and are truly willing to embrace the unknown, then we will come to rest. Everything will change. Our entire inner world and our relationship to life as a whole will turn upside down simply because we are ready and willing to stop struggling *forever*.

But there's more. If we're lucky, the peace that we have found through ceasing to struggle does not become yet another safe refuge, another fixed reference point. Instead it becomes that which gives us the courage to dive wholeheartedly into the experience of being fully alive. *It is very important to understand that going all the way means more than merely ceasing to struggle.* Going all the way means that *because* we have stopped struggling, we are finally able to dive fully into the experience of life. Why? Because we have given up all attachments to fixed ideas about peace and rest, we have found a willingness to struggle in a way that is entirely new. In fact, we find to our surprise that we experience a *calling* to struggle in a way that does not keep us bound, but literally sets the world on fire.

The discovery of this willingness makes something clear that shatters all of our ideas about Enlightenment: that final Liberation is found through caring more about life itself than in being free from it.

10

Hold onto Nothing

T he individual who is truly free has no idea who they are. If someone calls their name they will respond because they recognize that their name has been called, but they will not know who is responding. That is because this individual does not have any fixed notions of self.

What would it be like to realize a condition where one had no fixed notions of self? The answer is *undistracted*. Undistracted by the notion of being anyone or anything in particular. Undistracted by the personality and its endless stream of memories, fears and desires. Undistracted by all notions of self that relate to a Self Absolute. All notions of self, including ideas that represent that which is sacred, are an endless distraction in the eye of the mind. The formation of any image relating to self so easily obscures the limitless depth and subtlety that is always there.

It is only a rare individual who does not need to know who they are. And indeed this seems to be the greatest challenge if an individual wants to be free. We do not need to know who we are with our mind in any way to be able to be fully who we are in the most passionate way. In fact, we can only be who we are, as we are, unadorned by anything else, if we are free of *all* notions of self. It's impossible to be perfectly spontaneous, which is the true expression of a liberated personality, as long as we are distracted by any notion of self, relative or Absolute. Only if we have no idea who we are will we be able to find out who we are in each and every moment.

The spiritual journey is almost always supported in a fundamental way by concepts of self in which the seeker takes refuge. These concepts serve to create the illusion of safety in the chaotic ocean of life. It takes tremendous courage to embrace the possibility of being awake without needing to be supported by any notion of self, relative or Absolute. We do not need to add anything to what we are. We only need to endeavor to discover who and what we are, free from any fixed ideas.

If we are serious about awakening, it's imperative that sooner or later we come to terms with the fact that the significance of our personal history—everything that we have endured, pleasant and unpleasant, that makes us who we think we are in this moment—is utterly irrelevant in the face of the Truth. We have to find a way to directly perceive reality as it is, free from the corrupting influence of the mind. The mind will corrupt our interpretation of reality only if we allow it to do so. And we allow it to do so because we are frightened of the experience of no location, no point of reference, *no idea whatsoever.* If we are to find true spiritual freedom, then we have to find the way to remain completely free of any and all fixed notions of self that the mind can and will create. This is a constant endeavor.

The goal in the end is simply to see things as they are, to perceive reality as it is. We will know that we are beginning to arrive when we find that the personality is spontaneously expressing itself free from fear, free from any sense of limitation. When the personality becomes animated in such a way, we experience a condition in which we are constantly discovering actuality, always and ever new, free from any fixed reference point. That's what freedom is.

It is when we hold onto nothing that it is possible to know everything. There is no middle ground.

11

The Impersonal View

There is nothing personal about any aspect of your personal experience. Dare to become aware of the fact that every aspect of your personal experience is a completely impersonal affair. If you want to be free, I encourage you to look, to see and discover for yourself the ultimately impersonal nature of every single aspect of your personal experience. For some this may be obvious. But for most, to come to terms with the actuality of the fact that every single aspect of their personal experience is ultimately impersonal is very challenging indeed.

If you look deeply enough you will discover for yourself that in the end there is very little that is unique or special about any one of us. It is important to understand that ultimately there is only one body, there is only one mind and there is only one heart. It can be a very shocking experience to find out that so much of what it means to be alive is no more than a mechanical process. When you have the courage to penetrate beneath the surface and peer deeply into the impersonal dimension of life, you will be amazed at what you will find.

What creates so much of the conflict and chaos in our world is the staggering fact that almost every human being is convinced that they are unique, that they are special. Because so many of us have not penetrated beyond the superficial layers of our experience, we unwittingly cling onto the idea of being unique to find an identity, to locate a sense of self.

What is discovered in the spiritual experience that allows us to rest, that makes it possible to stop struggling against life, is the knowledge that every aspect of our personal experience is an impersonal affair. Indeed, the individual who has transcended the need to see themselves as being unique or special is instantly released from the tyranny of separation. It is this necessity to see ourselves as being unique or special that always takes us away from the truth of our ultimate nature and in that, away from everyone else. As long as we allow ourselves to be captivated by the emotional and psychological need to see ourselves as standing outside of and away from the whole, it will be impossible to truly come together with another. The more we are able to perceive the simple truth of the ultimately impersonal nature of all personal experience, the less we will feel compelled to see ourselves as being separate.

It requires an extraordinarily mature human being to bear the overwhelming implications of the revelation of impersonality. The individual who is able to do so sees through the illusion of separation that is created by the personalization of human experience. When the revelation of impersonality is perceived directly many are terrified— terrified because they feel that their personal relationship to their experience is being threatened. In that, they see for themselves how their personal relationship to so much of their experience has distorted the way things actually are. In light of this, they understand that so much of what appeared to be true is actually false. In fact, for most the Truth is too much to bear. It's too stark. It's too absolute. It is too overwhelming in its utter impersonality.

This recognition of the ultimate impersonality of all personal experience shows the way to the destruction of all false and wrong views about the nature of reality, relative and Absolute.

Dare to consider this question for yourself: *is there*

anything personal about any aspect of my personal experience?

Simply through the discovery of the impersonality of every aspect of your personal experience, you can find your own Liberation. That is all it takes. But to succeed, this demands a rare degree of interest and determination. This is not something to be done only during a period of meditation or reflection. It is not something to be done only at a particular time that one sets aside to pay attention. This is meant to be done always—when you are on the bus or when you are at work, when you experience anger or lust, when you are overwhelmed by sublime feelings, when you are profoundly happy. Whatever you could possibly think or feel, remember to ask yourself: is there anything personal about any aspect of my personal experience?

12

True Finders
Are Few

When you are on your own, where are you taking refuge? Most seekers are taking refuge somewhere. What ideas about yourself and what ideas about the Absolute are you taking refuge in?

If you want to be free, then you have to look into all of your beliefs. You have to find out who you *really* think you are.

Most seekers, knowingly or unknowingly, are ceaselessly cultivating a relationship between their individual sense of self and a larger idea of Self. So much of spiritual practice and experience is made up of the pursuit and cultivation of a relationship between an idea of a small self and an idea of a big Self, between an idea of man and an idea of God, between an idea of earth and an idea of heaven.

In fact, it is the pursuit and cultivation of this very relationship that is often believed to be the path to salvation.

Why is this a problem? Because unless the seeker finally comes to that point in their own evolution where they discover for themselves that *no relationship actually exists* between a small self and a big Self, between man and God, between earth and heaven, they will never become a true finder. Realizing this is so important. In fact, our success depends on it entirely. It is in profound understanding that the real meaning of spiritual freedom is known. In that understanding all relationship comes to an end.

True finders are few and far between. Indeed, most seekers prefer never to get this far. That is why the relationship between individuality and a larger, mysterious sense of Self is almost never gone beyond. Because in order to do so, *all ideas and beliefs which are places of refuge for the seeker have to be abandoned.*

It is only in the experiential discovery and unconditional acceptance of no relationship whatsoever that a Liberation that is final is born.

13

The Edge

Question Sooner or later, after being on the path for some time, you come to a place that feels like the edge of a cliff. From that place it seems that the only way to go farther is to take a leap, to abandon everything that you think you know. My question is: once you get to that place, how do you take that leap?

Answer If you've really come to that place, the question "How do I take that leap?" does not arise. But if you haven't come to the edge of that cliff, if you are a thousand miles away, then you may ask, "How do I do it? How do I take that leap?" But from a thousand miles away, there is no way to leap.

Q So how do you get there?

A   The way you get there is by becoming very serious. And the way to that seriousness is through asking yourself the two most fundamental spiritual questions as if your life depended on it: Who am I? and How shall I live?

You begin by asking yourself these two questions in a very sincere way. That means that you have come to the point where you have no doubt that your life literally depends upon finding the answers. When you discover a heartfelt urgency in relationship to these questions, you *are* walking towards the edge.

Most seekers dare to ask themselves serious questions at one time or another and in doing so begin to approach the edge of the cliff. But unfortunately too many get distracted along the way and lose touch with the all-important sense of urgency. Ambition, romance, fear and desire for security are the perennial distractions that ultimately foil all but the most sincere. The individual who is genuine in their desire to be free recognizes these distractions for what they are and does not allow themselves to become sidetracked. This is very rare.

When you get to the point where the edge can actually be seen, you will feel a magnetic current that literally seems to be pulling you to step beyond it. It's at those moments when you recognize in a way that is always shocking that the possibility of Liberation is *real*. You will then feel the intimations of your own death and simultaneously sense the dawning of no limitation. All fundamental beliefs about your identity and the nature of reality start to shake as you see this intellectually and feel it emotionally. You will experience an ever-growing pressure imposing itself on all of your fixed ideas. Indeed, as you get closer and closer to the edge, you recognize more and more directly just how vast and potentially unlimited the fact of being alive actually is.

At this point, many experience fear and what often proves to be overwhelming doubt. In the face of that which appears to be without limit, they see how small is almost all that they have been identified with. This is a shattering realization for the ego, an emotionally and intellectually crushing revelation that is absolutely terrifying. But if one has the rare courage to persevere in the face of the enormous temptation to doubt, one will not only be able to jump, but may never experience the need to hold on ever again.

You see, at the moment of letting go the question "How?" doesn't arise. There is only leaping into vastness.

Q And in that vastness you find the answers that you've been looking for?

A Yes. In a way that is final. That's the whole point. Along the way you may get glimpses. As you move closer and closer to that edge, you allow more and more of your attention to be attracted to what is on the other side, and as a result of that you will gain some insight into those questions. But those glimpses are in no way a final answer. They are moments of spiritual affirmation and confirmation. They say to you, "Yes, this is really true."

You see, even if one has had glimpses of revelation, one usually still experiences doubt. And under the pressure of that doubt, one's already delicate confidence can be shaken: "Is this all my imagination or is it real?"

Leaping off the edge means *a point of no return.* It's a place where doubt has been conquered forever. Some mistake mere glimpses along the way for that final leap. But they are not the same.

Q It's frightening to see how delicate all this is.

A Yes it is. And the reason it's frightening is because as you approach the edge, it becomes painfully obvious that you have nothing to gain from taking that leap, but in fact only have everything to lose. A lot of people hear the word "Enlightenment" and think, "It sounds like a great thing to have." But if you actually take that leap, you will lose everything. All that you thought you were has to be left behind on the edge of the cliff because you can't take anything with you when you jump. That's when you realize how shockingly real it is. That's when you find out that it's not a game.

14

Like a Twig in a Hurricane

Surrender means we don't know what's going to happen. When we surrender we give up needing to know. If surrender is genuine, that means in the very depths of our being we don't know what's going to happen.

Something extraordinary occurs when we allow ourselves the freedom to not know because it is then that everything opens up. It is then that the experience of life becomes profoundly joyous and unthinkably mysterious. Not knowing what's going to happen means ceasing to always insist upon knowing what the future will bring. When we surrender the need to know, we discover that things often work out in marvelous and unexpected ways that we could never have previously imagined. Only when we transcend the need to always be sure of what's going to happen in the future will there be room for that which is extraordinary and miraculous to reveal itself.

What would the experience of life be like if we were no longer seeking for any security whatsoever from the future? Everything would open up, everything would become possible. Why? Because we wouldn't be waiting any longer for the experience of life to become complete. When we realize that everything is possible, then the way we respond to life begins to break boundaries. All that was fixed is undone as that which was previously unthinkable becomes known. Many talk about surrender, but the truth is very few seem able to surrender to the degree necessary to achieve Liberation.

Genuine surrender is unconditional, absolute and always liberates. That means you have let go of everything to such a degree that you have found the very center of it all. You know, you see, you actually feel that that is where you abide—at the very center. True surrender means you have found it. You always know that that's where you are. Even physically you feel that that is where you abide.

The reason you are no longer preoccupied with the future is because the experience of life has become so rich, so full and so mysterious. If surrender is genuine, this revelation is always being reaffirmed. Over and over again you will recognize, "Yes, this is true." It's a knowing that is absolute, a knowing that is constantly being affirmed and reaffirmed.

Surrender is dynamic and explosive because it *is* Liberation. When you say, "Not my will but Thy will be done," and mean it, then something very big happens. The life of the personality comes to an end and a life that is truly unknown begins. If this has not happened in a way that is unmistakable, mysterious and profound, then one has not yet surrendered.

Only if you have let go to the degree that you feel your life is actually being taken away from you, literally swept away, can you know for sure that surrender has occurred. It's as if you have been picked up by a hurricane and thrown around like a little twig, having lost control of your destiny.

In the end, you will discover true happiness because you are not trying to hold on any longer. Indeed, it is ecstasy to be thrown around when you are not holding onto anything. Realize that it is only because you try to hold on that you suffer so much.

15

Perfect Aloneness

In the relationship with the spiritual teacher there is always the promise of no limitation. And it is the promise of no limitation that makes that relationship so interesting. But I've noticed that very few people take full advantage of the potential inherent in that relationship. Too many seek only to escape from having to be the one who is ultimately responsible for their own life. When an individual seeks only for escape in the relationship with the spiritual teacher, they are hoping to find some kind of security for themselves, and in that security, relief from the very challenging business of human existence. In merely seeking for security in the relationship with a spiritual teacher quite a lot can happen, but that relationship becomes truly powerful only when the individual is able to accept full responsibility for their own evolution. In doing so, one endeavors to meet the teacher in the teacher's perfect aloneness. That step, so few seem willing and interested in taking.

If the promise of no limitation inherent in the relationship with the spiritual teacher is to be fulfilled then the individual has to be ready and willing to meet the teacher absolutely and unconditionally. That means completely and without reservation. In this kind of meeting an unusual bond occurs. It's very difficult to describe. I'm making a distinction between a relationship that offers security for the ego and one that offers no security whatsoever for the ego. I'm describing a relationship that offers only perfect aloneness. That means perfect independence and the perfect fulfillment of one's individuality. What I'm pointing to is a rare and challenging possibility that is not often actualized.

In the initial meeting with the spiritual teacher it is not uncommon for one to have a powerful experience. One may have unusual feelings and sensations, and more importantly may experience profound insight that can and often does shake the very foundation of one's belief system. This may be such an extraordinary event that the individual might feel choicelessly drawn to enter into an intimate relationship with the one in the presence of whom they realized so much. But what too often seems to happen is that instead of using that initial experience as a catalyst from which to find their own Liberation, unknowingly the individual assumes a safe and secure position in that experience and rests in it. Indeed, it is only the rare individual who genuinely aspires for Liberation and not dependence in the relationship with the spiritual teacher.

All seek for affirmation. All want to hear that they are alright, to feel that everything is okay. In the beginning stages of association and relationship with the spiritual teacher, it's reasonable to seek for a very profound affirmation of oneself, and in that to experience a deep healing on an emotional level. The intense experiences that the individual may have upon meeting the spiritual teacher act as that affirmation, that healing. But most choose to rest there.

It's important that the experience of healing and affirmation that often occurs in the meeting with the spiritual teacher serve not as a resting place but as the foundation for a Liberation that is profound. That means that that meeting should be a simultaneous ending of the past and beginning of an unusual and very different future. That future is the sincere and intense pursuit of dissolution—the dissolution of all false and wrong views about the nature of reality, relative and Absolute—and finally the resurrection of a human personality that is free from the profound limitations that are the inevitable consequence of being lost in delusion and ignorance.

A sincere individual should be willing to give everything to be able to manifest and express that freedom as a living breathing possibility, *as themselves*. This order of approach to spiritual life is very different than one of merely seeking for some kind of security and safety in the presence of a powerful human being.

The individual I'm speaking about is finally going to end up only with themselves. Because the one who wants to go all the way strives to meet the spiritual teacher in perfect aloneness, in perfect isolation. That's something very different than what most seekers are actually looking for.

16

A Trust That
Is Absolute

The spiritually awakened condition is one in which the individual has realized a trust that is absolute. What is extraordinary about this condition is that in it there is no difference between the experience of trust in the personal self and trust in life itself. This attainment of nonduality and perfect wholeness forces those who are sincere to question fundamental beliefs about barriers that have been created in the eye of the mind. The barriers between self and other, self and world all come into question when one contemplates the liberating implications of experiencing a trust that is absolute.

Looking at the human condition in relationship to the highest possibility of perfect Liberation, one finds that it is the presence of trust that destroys all boundaries and all notions of separation. In fact, the literal demonstration of an absolute principle is the experience of and ability to manifest a trust that is absolute, a trust in which the division between the personal self and the absolute principle has been destroyed. When an individual is able to sustain this attainment with unbroken consistency, something sacred has occurred.

The liberating power of absolute trust cannot and will not reveal itself as long as the need to remain separate, isolated and alone, apart from the other and apart from the totality of life is tolerated. Indeed, only when the need to remain separate has died once and for all will the liberating power of absolute trust become manifest in this world in such a way that demonstrates the living presence of an absolute principle. It is the power of a trust that is absolute that makes all things possible. In its presence the distinction between heaven and earth, nirvana and samsara is destroyed. When absolute trust is found there will be nothing more to attain, because literally nothing will exist between the personal self and the rest of life.

17

Integrity Is Multidimensional

The spiritual process is an evolutionary one—a movement towards wholeness, a movement towards integrity. The expression of a liberated condition is integrity, in the most fundamental sense of the word, which means perfectly undivided. From an evolutionary point of view, the seeker is striving to realize their full humanity. They are trying to discover, come to terms with and ultimately be able to manifest what it means to be a liberated—which means integrated—human being.

It is important to understand that when a human being strives to realize integrity, the struggle to come to the end of division within themselves cannot be seen in isolation, but must be recognized as being nonseparate from the evolutionary struggle that the whole race is lost in. Indeed, the one who sincerely aspires for Liberation must struggle with the very same forces within themselves that keep humanity divided against itself.

Victory in the quest for Liberation is the attainment of a final integrity. And that attainment is dependent upon the discovery of a fundamental perfection that is always there, if only one had the eyes to see it. The essence of that perfection is order, the fundamental order of the universe itself. The one who is victorious has recognized their own identity as nonseparate from that perfection/order. It is through the direct experiential discovery of that perfection/order that Liberation from a deeply divided condition is won. And it is through that discovery alone that one ceases to blindly struggle. Against what? Against the fundamental perfection/order that has always been there.

The fact is that few come upon this perfection/order for more than brief moments. And of those who do, there are even fewer who realize the vision of this perfection/order to such a degree that their own lives are able to demonstrate a seamless expression of it. From a spiritual perspective, the implications of integrity are always multidimensional because not only does integrity correspond to the individual's moral and ethical relationship to life, but it simultaneously also corresponds to the depth of that individual's knowledge of the inherent perfection/order that lies at the root of all that is.

The attainment of a final integrity proves that it is possible to become a liberated human being—a liberated human being in a world where for the most part the human condition is and has been an expression of the very opposite of that.

18

Spiritual Conscience

In the spiritual experience, we discover something very important. We find that who and what we are cannot be limited to a particular group of events that have historical points of reference. Indeed, we come face-to-face with the fact that who and what we are cannot be confined by the movement of time. In that experience we know without any doubt that we are not separate from the whole, and it is that discovery that can liberate us from believing ourselves to be an isolated, self-contained entity. Not only can we find personal liberation in that experience, but we also may find something else that is far more significant, which is a profound sense of responsibility for the whole.

This sense of responsibility for the whole that can be awakened through the spiritual experience is what I call spiritual conscience. When this conscience has been found, we will finally be able to see clearly the obvious relationship that has always existed between self and other, self and world. And it is because of this that we will begin to see for ourselves unequivocally that our own actions as a human being have countless effects that spread out in all directions. When we discover the spiritual conscience, we will find to our amazement that we are able to perceive the terrifying delicacy of what it means to be a human being who is awake.

To be awake means that we are no longer hiding from the unavoidable fact of interrelatedness. If we are truly awake, our actions will express the fact that we are taking into consideration the consequences of the choices we are making in a way that demonstrates that the boundaries of the personal have been destroyed forever.

Spiritual experience is meaningless unless in that experience a sense of responsibility that transcends the boundaries of the personal has been discovered. In fact, what makes the spiritual experience truly significant is not only that this conscience has been found; what alone gives it value is the degree of courage we have to respond to that which it reveals to us. That which it reveals to us is always overwhelming in its implications. But if we are able to respond wholeheartedly and without reservation, not only will we discover our own Liberation as a result, but to our surprise we will also find that the whole world has been saved.

19

This Mysterious Secret

Q *uestion*   How do you know if your actions are the right ones?

Answer   All anyone has to do if they want to see how appropriate their actions really are, is to look back. Anybody can do this. All you have to do is turn around and look behind you—at the last two weeks, the last two months, the last two years. Look and see for yourself how profound, how liberated is the expression of your own life. That is how you can know.

Q   Do you mean to say there is no way in the midst of acting to tell if your response is the right one?

A   Yes, exactly. You will be able to tell only by looking back. You see, we never have time to be completely sure in the present moment. Sometimes we think we know what we are doing. This can either turn out to be true or it can become clear that we were self-deceived. In the end, the only way to tell is through seeing what actually occurs. All we have in the moment that we act is that we feel sure, or intuitively that it feels right, or that it simply seems to make sense.

Indeed, there are moments in life when we feel compelled to act because everything tells us that we're doing the right thing. For example, you're on the beach with a person who you feel attracted to. The moon is out. You hear the sound of the ocean and feel the wind in your face. There is a powerful feeling rising up from within that says, "YES." You feel it, the other person feels it. Your heart is beating, your body is screaming. Suddenly it seems that the whole universe is saying, "YES, YES, YES!" There's no doubt to be found anywhere. But the next morning you may say, "Oh my God. What have I done?"

The way we feel in any given moment is not necessarily always a reliable indication of what the most appropriate response is. In that moment there is no way we can be completely sure. To be sure we need time. Time must pass in order to know what the most appropriate response would have been. The more time, the better. In the end, you can only tell by looking back. This is the frightening truth. If you are serious about your own Liberation, you will strive to come to that point where, when you look back, what you will see is on a fundamental level without error. Indeed, what you will see is the expression of something that is wholesome, profound, perfect and mysterious. Strive to get to the point where the trail you leave behind you is the expression of a rare consistency of pure motivation that continually has profound effects and wholesome consequences.

Q But if one discovers that one's perception of the present can't be trusted, then how could one's perception of what has happened in the past be trusted?

A I didn't say that one's perception of the present can't be trusted. I said that you can't be completely sure.

Q Then how could you be sure of what has happened in the past?

A You can be sure when it becomes apparent in looking

back that the consistency that I just described has been manifesting itself in an unbroken manner over a significant period of time. Then trust will arise naturally. Indeed, you will begin to trust yourself in a way that was previously unimaginable. Why? Because you will see that it is happening by itself over and over again—a consistency that is the expression of pure motivation. If when you look back that is what you see and it is also what many others see, then the trust that you asked about will be there. The fact is that in the present moment you never can be completely sure how to respond in the most perfect manner, but you have to respond anyway. If you want to live fully, you have to be able to respond to life *right now*. To freely respond in the present moment, the security of always being sure will not be available to you.

Q But where is it that pure motivation comes from?

A Pure motivation comes from precisely that place where it is not possible to be sure, a place beyond all pairs of opposites. Indeed, what results from going beyond all pairs of opposites, beyond good and bad, beyond right and wrong is goodness, perfect goodness. That's the whole point. You see, from not being sure mysteriously arises the expression of a pure motivation and perfect consistency, the consequences of which are always profound. Very few people know about this mysterious secret.

It's because we experience so much insecurity that we so badly want to come to a point where we can say, "Now I'm sure, now I can relax." But what is fascinating is that for that kind of relaxation and the confidence that comes from a deep trust in life to become manifest in a way that is profound, we have to find a way to be more and more comfortable with not being sure.

20

The Personalization of Feeling

Without a doubt, the most difficult arena of human experience, the place where almost all get perilously lost, is in the experience of feeling. The reason for this is a tendency to personalize almost every experience of feeling that arises. This tendency is a blind and conditioned habit that has become so automatic that most are unable to see beyond it. It is this tendency to personalize almost every feeling that arises that makes it so difficult for human beings to realize a perspective upon their experience of feeling that is truly objective.

One of the greatest challenges for any human being who wants to be free is faced when they dare to step beyond the experience of feeling. Stepping beyond the experience of feeling means allowing oneself to perceive directly the ultimately impersonal nature of *all* feeling experience. To do this, every single idea and belief one has ever had about what feelings mean in relationship to the personality has to be suspended. If this can be done successfully, one will be amazed at what one will find. One will be able to see maybe for the very first time how conditioned, how empty of personal significance, how truly *impersonal* so much of our experience of feeling actually is.

For most of us this fact is hard to bear. Because in light of it, the illusion of so much of what we believe to be personal becomes apparent very quickly. Indeed, what is revealed is a picture that is very stark. What we find is that on the level of feeling, so much of human experience is utterly identical in nature and under close scrutiny proves itself to be empty of any unique attributes that could indicate anything special about the experiencer. What most human beings seem to be unaware of is the fact that they seek to locate a sense of personal identity in a domain of human experience that is, in and of itself, devoid of any quality that could be called personal.

One has to be ready to see this, and one will only be ready if one has no doubt that one wants to be free. Otherwise one will always be afraid of real depth, afraid of going too deeply into spiritual experience, of going so deep that even the personal significance of the experience of feeling falls away.

The difference between bondage and Liberation is always black and white and the challenge of profound Liberation from unending confusion is unconditional. As long as we are invested in a relationship to our feeling experience that is anything other than fully liberated, a perspective upon that experience that has the power to free us from the unending confusion that feeling experience creates will always be too challenging to accept.

21

A Love So Great

Question You have said that we cannot measure how free we are by how we feel or what we think. So how can we finally determine whether we are free or not?

Answer How free we are can be determined by how much love we are able to manifest.

Q What does that actually mean?

A What that means is how much delusion about the nature of love, truth and self we are able to destroy in others.

Q I thought you were going to say "within ourselves."

A "Within ourselves" is a very dubious arena. It's hard to tell what "within ourselves" actually means. In the end, you can only find out what is going on within yourself by the depth of intimacy and unshakable trust that you are able to demonstrate in your relationships with other people. When all is said and done, that is the only way you will be able to determine clearly what is happening inside yourself. Otherwise there is no way to tell for sure.

Don't you see, if we want to be free then we must be sincere about destroying all of the boundaries that keep us separate. If we are sincere we will ultimately discover that those boundaries are only personal. It is with that recognition that the profoundly limited way that we relate to self, other and life as a whole can be completely transformed.

Q In what way?

A In such a way that when you are associating with others, you are no longer relating in a manner that is fundamentally personal. Why? Because you have realized a love that is so great that by its sheer magnitude a relationship that was based on that which could be called personal could never contain it. What this means is that you are now no longer so preoccupied with the history, gender or age of the other. Now you are primarily interested in the mystery of Self that constantly reveals itself to be the only Truth in every moment. When all else becomes secondary, it is this that becomes apparent.

The kind of love I'm speaking about has nothing to do with time, with history, with that which is personal. This kind of love contains no trace of sentimentality. If you are compelled to respond to this kind of love then believe me, your so-called personal life will become transformed in a way that is unimaginable. This love and the power of its demand for absolute submission to itself is far too destructive to all that is false for most to bear. Indeed, this kind of submission has to be something one is already intuitively attracted to, otherwise it will never be recognized for what it truly is: an unconditional demand from a love that is absolute. Unadorned, undistorted by fear and uncorrupted by desire, make no mistake about it, true love threatens every false notion we have about self, life and reality as a whole. True love threatens absolutely *everything*. This is the highest form of love.

Again, what I'm speaking about has no relationship to a love that is merely personal. Sentimental feelings and our attachment to them will always only reveal themselves to be agents of a separate existence. Love that is transcendent is impersonal and cares not about that which is personal. This is a big, big stretch and difficult for most to truly grasp. The question "What is in that kind of love for me?" is often the unstated but deeply felt response. The answer is *nothing.* This is why I rarely speak about love. Because I know that when I use that word, what is most often thought of has nothing to do with the kind of love that I'm pointing to.

True love has everything to do with relationship, with that magnetic force that draws us together. Love that is free from that which is personal purifies *unconditionally.* Like fire—it burns. We must be willing and ready to be consumed by this fire, otherwise we will say, "This is too much for me."

Q   What is it like to be in a relationship with one who has realized the depth of love you are speaking about?

A   Overwhelming in its intensity, absolute in its demand.

Q   But does this intensity have the power to pull others up to its level?

A   Yes, of course it does. But more likely it will send people running. It all depends upon how far one wants to go. For the uninitiated, the reason that the power of this kind of love is so disarming is that within its parameters falsehood cannot survive. The quickest way to lose those you think you love the most is through discovering true love. You see, so many of us hide in relationships that are based on that which is false, superficial and ultimately insubstantial. But if we truly desire Liberation, then we will seek for the kind of relationships with others in which it would be impossible to hide. This will help to understand the way in which spiritual awakening directly affects the depth and quality of the relationships we have with others.

Q   What is it exactly that would compel us to run from true love?

A   Fear of truth. Fear of recognizing falsehood. The overwhelming fear of being truly free. That is why so many of us are so deeply invested in seeing that which is limited in a much bigger light than it actually is. If we truly want to be free, we will find a strength of intention within ourselves that will protect us from the temptation to escape into falsehood. We will be unwilling to see that which is unreal as real and that which is false as true. Because we will know that in the end, there is no escape.

22

Ecstatic Intimacy

Q *uestion* Why would one choose to come together with other people in spiritual community rather than try to reach Enlightenment on one's own through meditation or contemplation?

Answer Unbearable intimacy. Can you imagine that? *Unbearable ecstatic intimacy.*

You see, without realizing it people tenaciously cling to an idea of being unique or special, which in this case means separate. In fact, most human beings suffer from this compulsive need to see themselves as being separate. What I'm speaking about is an aggressive psychological habit that makes it possible for the individual to always see themselves as standing outside of and away from the whole. This habit is called self-consciousness.

If one is very invested in seeing oneself as being unique or special, coming together in ecstatic intimacy with others would not seem like an attractive idea but in fact would appear as a threat. Indeed, the idea itself would make one feel that one couldn't breathe because in that intimacy there would be no room left for oneself. But that's the whole point. The whole point is to die to that need to see oneself as being separate in any way.

Dying to that need to see oneself as being separate reveals a completely new experience which is intimacy, ecstatic intimacy. This discovery, the discovery of the ecstasy that comes from the experiential recognition of the nondifference between self and other, does not only arise from the experience of internal revelation. Miraculously, it can be experienced simply through being together with another.

What would it be like to feel no gap of time, no gap of space, no gap of doubt with another? It's very difficult to imagine because the experience of perfect trust hardly exists in the world that we live in. What would it be like if one person could truly come together with another? What would it be like if a handful of people could come together in such a way that there was no gap whatsoever, where one was able to trust implicitly the good intentions of the other?

If that was possible one would find oneself in a completely different world. One's experience of what it would mean to be a human being would be very, very different.

When one is psychologically and emotionally freed from the relentless burden of always needing to see oneself as being separate, one discovers the true Self—the Self we all are when we are undistracted by the need to see ourselves as being separate in any way. That discovery is ecstasy itself. In that discovery we come to rest. In that discovery there is no fear and no wanting—only love, freedom and joy. Why? Because one is resting in one's true nature.

Now if that experience could become manifest in a way that was collective, then in that event all that is false, wrong and untrue in this world would be defeated. In that event, the very essence of the problem with the world in which we live, which is the need to remain separate, would be destroyed. Then our true Self that is transcendent and completely impersonal can express itself *as ourselves.* That's when the miracle of unity becomes manifest in a way that is self-evident. In that unity everything is revealed. Instantly one understands not only why things are the way they are, but even more importantly how things can be. Suddenly everything begins to make sense in the recognition of why we are here—to prove that it is possible.

You have to understand, what I'm pointing to far transcends in significance the Liberation of the individual alone. One individual's success in and of itself is not enough. For evolution to occur in a way that is truly significant there must be a collective victory. A collective victory in which many individuals are simultaneously consciously living in the knowledge of their true Self. Only then have we succeeded.

23

An Immaculate Condition

What distinguishes a person who is awake from someone who is not is that they are able to recognize that which is true. Someone who is awake is able to see much more of what is actually there than someone who is not. This is because the quality of their attention has become vast, subtle and profound.

The word "Enlightenment" does not only refer to the awareness of being or to the experience of bliss. Enlightenment means being aware of what is always right in front of us. If we seek only to acquire a specific experience, a particular feeling, a certain spiritual event, then we will not necessarily become enlightened. The reason for that is because we will always only be focused on a fixed idea about what it is that we are looking for.

The goal is to realize a condition in which with all of our being all we want to know is that which is true. At the same time, in that condition emotionally we are not attached in any way to what that truth should be. I'm speaking about realizing a condition in which our deepest desire is simply to know what's true *for its own sake.* That means we want to know, from the depths of our being we want to know. But in that passion to know there are no fixed ideas about that which will be known. When we come to that point where we want to know what is true more than anything else and hold no fixed ideas, there will be room to find out what is actually true.

But there is more. Even when we discover that which is true, the desire to know that which is true for its own sake *must remain constant.* That means that even when we do know, we still do not shift from our original position. Even then we still only want to know what is true. That's why we never rest. Because in spite of the fact that we have discovered that which is true, we do not become fixed. We still only want to know what is true.

Once again, in that passion to know there can be no fixed ideas. We simply see, and the conclusions drawn about what is being seen are based on that which is living and present. For revelation to have liberating power it must be *living*. In order for revelation to remain alive, that condition in which we are attached to no fixed ideas must be our own.

In such a condition it not only becomes possible to realize that which is true, but it is that very condition that makes it possible to *always* know that which is true. Again, that condition is one where our most fundamental desire and longing is a passionate interest in what is true for its own sake. And that passion must be supported by no fixed ideas whatsoever. If it's any other way, even if we do discover that which is true, our interpretation of our experience will always be corrupted by those ideas. That is the difference between religion that is dead and revelation that is alive.

This matter is delicate. Only if you passionately want to know what is true, and at the same time have the courage and fearless interest to not impose any fixed or rigid ideas upon that which is discovered, have you realized a condition that could be called immaculate. It is this, the immaculate condition, that makes it possible to know that which is ever new.

24

Final Purity

There is a way to respond to life that is always miraculous, that is free from fear and that always transcends the mind's ability to grasp or understand. Indeed, responding to life in the way that I'm speaking about demands that we know how to act in such a way that moves faster than any form of premeditation would allow. Learning this secret enables us to endlessly discover a mystery that cannot be imagined.

To be able to live in this way that is always miraculous, we must be willing to be in a state of not knowing. That means we have to be ready to embrace a kind of austerity that is relentless. This austerity is the unconditional renunciation of the *need* to know. Indeed, there can be no final purity in any spiritual attainment unless one can do this perfectly. Purity can become manifest only when one is able to live without reservation in that knowledge that one doesn't know and will *never* know.

I'm describing a way of living that most would consider strange, nonsensical and even dangerous. You see, one discovers that one doesn't need to know in order to be able to function *perfectly*. That's the miracle, that's the mystery and that is what is extraordinary about this.

25

What Would You Do?

hat would you do if you realized it was all up to you? What would you do if suddenly you realized that the entire evolution of the whole human race rested on *your shoulders alone?* What would you do?

Take a risk and let yourself go. Simply imagine. Imagine you are sitting alone on a crowded bus. You're on your way to work. Then for no apparent reason everything becomes quiet. You are no longer able to hear any sound. All the voices around you disappear. Then it becomes even more dramatic. Now you are not able to see anything or anyone. Everything disappears. Suddenly you find yourself overwhelmed by a blazing white light. In every direction all you can see is dazzling radiance. In your ever-growing bewilderment, you find yourself being informed by an unseen presence that the evolution of the entire human race rests on your shoulders alone. Then as quickly as it came, it all vanishes. Dazed, you find yourself back on the crowded bus surrounded by other passengers on their way to work.

If this happened to you what would you do? Would you be able to avoid the overwhelming implications of a call from the Absolute? Would this realization have a profound impact on your relationship to the movement of your own mind? Would it affect your relationship to the way you feel from one moment to another? Would this shocking revelation have any impact on the way you relate to the past, the present and the future? Would your relationship to life and all of your experience change in a way that was unequivocal, or are you so lost in the drama of your own personal life that you would be able to remain the same? Indeed, would it still be possible for you to sustain the validity of a frighteningly self-centered relationship to life?

The only way for this miserable world to truly change is when the individual is willing to go beyond the personal in a way that is nothing less than heroic. Anything less will allow us to remain in a condition of always wanting only for ourselves. Like a beggar we will live a tortured existence in a perpetual state of need. This is the way most of us are willing to live our lives.

In order to be able to live up to the liberating idealism that many of us have experienced clearly at one time or another we have to be ready to assume a great burden, and that burden is the evolution of the whole. Because to succeed, we must be prepared to do battle with the powerful conditioning, conscious and unconscious, of the whole race. That means we have to come out from behind the shadows and be seen. Like Atlas, we have to be willing to hold up the whole world on our own shoulders. It's an awesome task.

So if something very unusual happened to you, what would you do?

Andrew Cohen is not just a spiritual teacher—he is an inspiring phenomenon. Since his awakening in 1986 he has only lived, breathed and spoken of one thing: the potential of total liberation from the bondage of ignorance, superstition and self-ishness. Powerless to limit his unceasing investigation, he has looked at the "jewel of enlightenment" from every angle, and given birth to a teaching that is vast and subtle, yet incomparably direct and revolutionary in its impact.

Through his public teachings, his books and his meetings with spiritual leaders of almost every tradition, he has tirelessly sought to convey his discovery that spiritual liberation's true significance is its potential to completely transform not only the individual, but the entire way that human beings, as a race, live together. In sharp contrast to the cynicism which is so pervasive today, yet with full awareness of the difficult challenges that we face, he has dared to teach and to show that it is indeed possible to bring heaven to earth. This powerful message of unity, openness and love has inspired many who have heard it to join together to prove its reality with their own lives, igniting an ever-expanding international revolution of tremendous vitality and significance.

Other Titles from Moksha Press

Enlightenment Is a Secret

Enlightenment Is a Secret, a collection of dialogues and essays taken from the teachings of Andrew Cohen, is a manual for personal liberation. This remarkable work explores every question crucial to the spiritual quest in a timeless and deeply illuminating way. Each excerpt is a meditation on emptiness which always brings the reader to a depth greater than the mind can grasp. Love, renunciation, surrender, humility, detachment, the mind, spiritual practice and many other topics are addressed with a clarity so powerful that it constantly challenges the reader to go further and further. One of the most original expressions of awakened understanding by a western teacher in our time, *Enlightenment Is a Secret* is a book for endless study and contemplation, and potentially a door to genuine liberation. ($14.95)

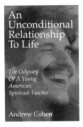

An Unconditional Relationship to Life

This fourth book by Andrew Cohen is a strikingly original and powerfully experiential journey through the modern spiritual world both East and West. Describing the evolution of his own understanding through his meetings with teachers from various traditions, Andrew weaves an expose that is surprising in that it is simultaneously provocative and uplifting. Through questioning many of the current spiritual paradigms, he opens a door to a deeper understanding, revealing what the goal of liberation actually is, unencumbered by the usual myths and superstitions which are so rampant in the spiritual world today. Andrew's bold call to think independently challenges the reader to look beyond that which may have become all too familiar in a way that both inspires and liberates. ($10.95)

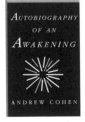

Autobiography of an Awakening

Autobiography of an Awakening is a portrayal of Andrew Cohen's uncompromising search for liberation, his profound awakening, and finally his painful struggle to come to terms with the discrepancy between his teacher's realization and his own. As he attempts to make sense out of the confusing conduct of his teacher, Andrew is forced to question again and again the real meaning and significance of the enlightened condition. The result is a disarmingly personal story, and a fascinating investigation into the causes of the corruption so prevalent in the spiritual world today. *Autobiography of an Awakening* is a powerful work that reveals both the explosive implications of what it means to aspire to spiritual liberation and the extraordinary dedication that it takes for any human being to stand alone in the truth. ($10.95)

An Absolute Relationship to Life

What would it mean to have an absolute relationship to the entire experience of being alive? In this compelling teaching, Andrew Cohen asks us to consider this possibility–a possibility which is ultimately challenging yet profoundly freeing. With piercing clarity, he describes how most human beings live their entire lives lost in the experience of thought, enslaved by the experience of feeling and trapped by the movement of time. Andrew explains that as long as this is the case we will never know what it means to be fully alive and points us toward an unequivocal and absolute shift in the way we relate to all of our experience. Culminating in a liberating revelation of what life would actually be like if we make this shift, this book challenges us to look directly into our own experience to find out for ourselves what an absolute relationship to life could truly be. ($6.00)

The Challenge of Enlightenment

This book, taken from an historic talk given in Bodhgaya, India in January 1996, illuminates the totality and depth of the path to liberation. Explaining that most of us are only aware of half of life, the world of action, Andrew Cohen guides us to sink below the surface of our experience to discover the world of inaction, of stillness, the very essence of who we are. Opening up a vast space inside us, this realization ultimately reveals the way for us to return once again to the world of action as an undivided, fully human being. To return to the world as we know it without losing touch with the depth that we have realized is the challenge of enlightenment. ($6.00)

My Master Is My Self

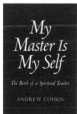

My Master Is My Self is the compelling story of one man's single-hearted dedication to the discovery of the truth and the profound spiritual realization that irrevocably transformed his life. It begins with an intimate account of the meeting between Andrew Cohen and the then little-known Indian teacher H.W.L. Poonja, which catapulted the author into an explosive spiritual awakening. As this extraordinary love story between teacher and student unfolds, the diaries and letters that compose this book go on to chronicle the events that ensued in Andrew's life during the next three years, describing the evolution of his understanding and how his own teaching began. Having come to be regarded as a modern underground spiritual classic, *My Master Is My Self* is a timeless work which portrays with captivating passion and rare depth the unfolding of a remarkable awakening and the birth of a profound spiritual teaching. ($10.95)

Books are available at bookstores or directly from Moksha Press:
P.O. Box 2360, Lenox, MA 01240 USA • Tel: 800-376-3210 or 413-637-6000 • Fax: 413-637-6015
Add $3 shipping for each book ordered. Please call for a free catalog.

For more information about Andrew Cohen and his teaching please contact:

Moksha Foundation - *a nonprofit organization founded in 1988 to support and facilitate the teaching work of Andrew Cohen. It is dedicated to the enlightenment of the individual and the expression of enlightenment in the world.*

FACE - *Friends of Andrew Cohen Everywhere represents the larger body of Andrew Cohen's students who have come together to try to manifest sanity in an insane world.*

North America

MOKSHA FOUNDATION and
INTERNATIONAL CENTER FOR FACE
P.O. Box 2360
Lenox, MA 01240 USA
tel: 800-376-3210 or 413-637-6000
fax: 413-637-6015
email: moksha@moksha.org
website: http://www.moksha.org

FACE BOSTON
2269 Massachusetts Avenue
Cambridge, MA 02140 USA
tel: 617-492-2848
fax: 617-876-3525
email: 73214.602@compuserve.com

FACE TORONTO
167 Spadina Road
Toronto, Ontario, Canada M5R 2T9
tel: 416-944-8175
fax: 416-964-8137
email: 104361.536@compuserve.com

FACE NEW YORK
tel: 212-978-4275
email: info@faceny.org

Europe

FACE LONDON
Centre Studios
Englands Lane
London NW3 4YD UK
tel: 44-171-483-3732
fax: 44-171-916-3170
email: 100074.3662@compuserve.com

FACE AMSTERDAM
Sarphatistraat 70
1018 GR Amsterdam, Holland
tel: 31-20-639-2501
fax: 31-20-639-1417
email: 100412.160@compuserve.com

FACE COLOGNE
Elsassstrasse 69
50677 Cologne, Germany
tel: 49-221-310-1040
fax: 49-221-331-9439
email: 100660.1375@compuserve.com

Other Centers

FACE TEL AVIV
8 Remez Street
Tel Aviv, Israel 62096
tel: 972-3695-3697
fax: 972-3691-6828
email: 100274.3277@compuserve.com

FACE SYDNEY
479 Darling Street
Balmain, Sydney
NSW 2041 Australia
tel/fax: 61-2-9555-2932
email: 105312.2467@compuserve.com